Conrad K. Butler

THE LIFE OF CATS - AMAZING FACTS

children's book

Copyright 2023©

1. CATS MAKE ABOUT 100 DIFFERENT SOUNDS, DOGS ONLY ABOUT 10.

2. PEOPLE WHO ARE ALLERGIC
TO CATS ARE NOT ALLERGIC
TO THEIR HAIR, BUT TO CAT
SALIVA OR TO PARTICLES OF
EPIDERMIS DEPOSITED ON
THE FUR.

3. CATS DON'T RECOGNIZE THE SWEET TASTE.

6. CATS DO NOT HAVE A COLLARBONE. THIS "LACK" MEANS THAT THEY CAN PRESS INTO ANY GAPS THEIR HEAD CAN PASS THROUGH.

5. CATS ONLY SWEAT ON THE SOLES OF THEIR PAWS.

6. EACH CAT'S NOSE
IS AS UNIQUE
AS A HUMAN
FINGERPRINT.

7. MALE CATS ARE USUALLY LEFT-HANDED AND FEMALE CATS ARE MORE LIKELY TO USE THEIR RIGHT PAW.

8. MOST WHITE CATS WITH BLUE EYES ARE DEAF. WHITE CATS WITH ONLY ONE EYE BLUE ARE DEAF TO THE EAR ON THE SIDE OF THE BLUE EYE.

9. A CAT CANNOT SEE WHAT IS DIRECTLY IN FRONT OF ITS NOSE. THEREFORE, HE OFTEN CANNOT FIND SMALL PIECES (E.G. FOOD) ON THE FLOOR.

10. THERE ARE 230 BONES IN A CAT'S BODY, AND 206 IN A HUMAN'S BODY.

11. A CAT CAN HEAR SOUNDS UP TO TWO OCTAVES HIGHER THAN A HUMAN HEARS.

12. THE CAT'S VIEWING ANGLE IS APPROXIMATELY 185 DEGREES.

13. ALMOST 10% OF ALL BONES OF A CAT ARE IN ITS TAIL.

14. CATS CAN SEE UP TO 36 METERS.

15. MOST LITTERS HAVE FROM 1 TO 9 KITTENS. THERE WERE 19 KITTENS IN THE RECORD LITTER, OF WHICH 15 SURVIVED.

16. CATS HAVE SO-CALLED THIRD EYELID. IT PREVENTS DRY EYES AND OTHER DAMAGE FROM OCCURRING.

17. THE CAT'S SPINE IS VERY FLEXIBLE, BECAUSE IT CONSISTS OF AS MANY AS 53 LOOSELY CONNECTED VERTEBRAE. THE HUMAN SPINE HAS ONLY 3L VERTEBRAE.

18. A CAT'S JAW DOES NOT MOVE SIDEWAYS, WHICH IS WHY CATS ARE UNABLE TO CHEW LARGE CHUNKS OF FOOD.

19. CATS USUALLY HAVE
12 WHISKERS ON EACH SIDE
OF THEIR FACE.

20. THE MAXIMUM SPEED
WHEN RUNNING THE CAT
IS 30 MPH.

21. CHEETAHS ARE THE ONLY CATS THAT DO NOT HIDE THEIR CLAWS.

22. CATS ARE EXTREMELY SENSITIVE TO VIBRATIONS AND VIBRATIONS. APPARENTLY, THEY CAN SENSE AN IMPENDING EARTHQUAKE 10-15 MINUTES BEFORE A PERSON.

23. CATS CAN EASILY CLIMB TREES, BUT GOING DOWN TO THE GROUND IS A PROBLEM FOR THEM BECAUSE THE HOOKED CLAWS ARE BENT ONLY ONE WAY.

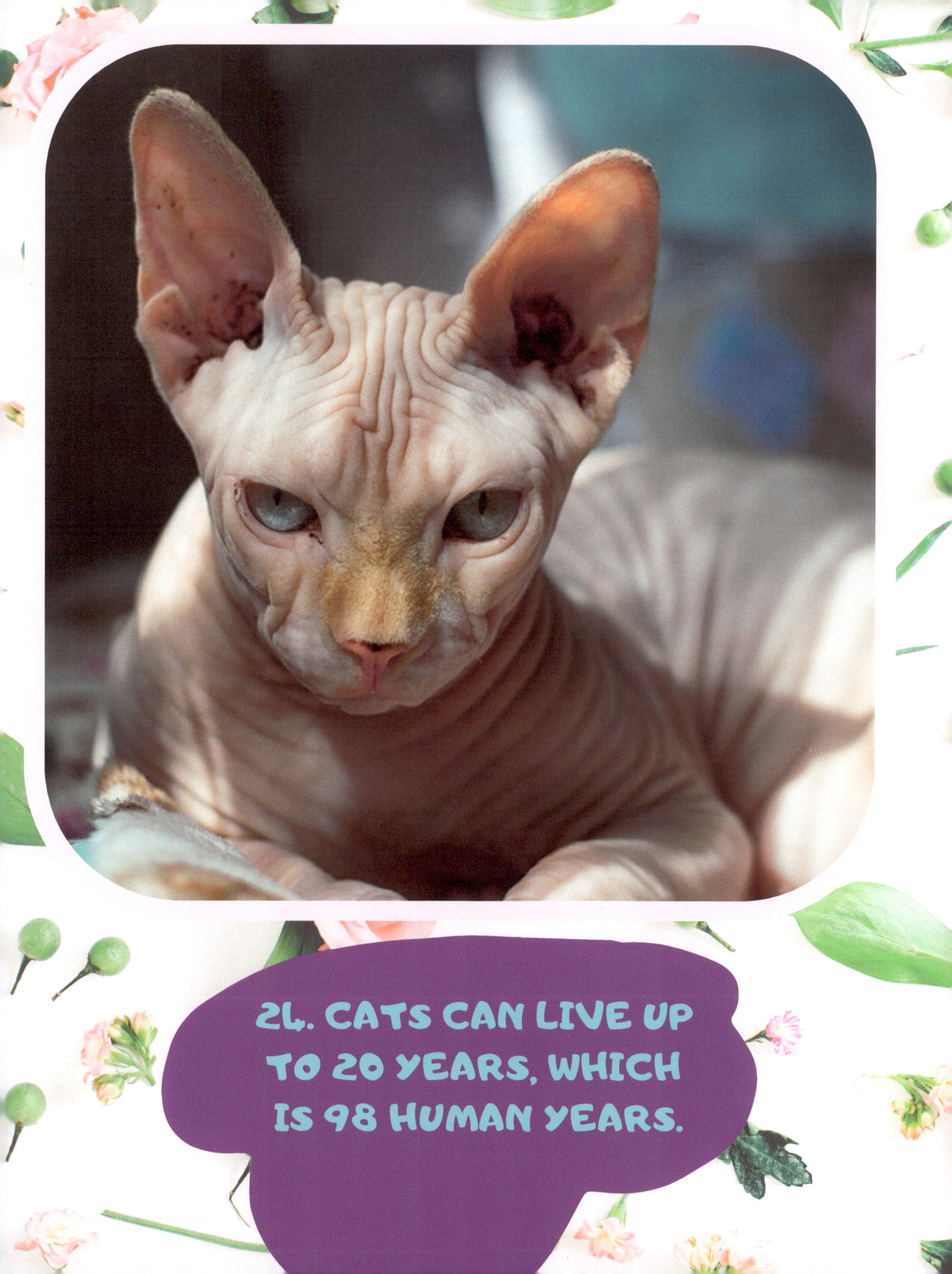
24. CATS CAN LIVE UP
TO 20 YEARS, WHICH
IS 98 HUMAN YEARS.

25. CATS USE THEIR WHISKERS TO "SENSE" THE WORLD AROUND THEM, TRYING TO FIGURE OUT WHAT SMALL SPACES THEY CAN FIT INTO.

26. THE AVERAGE CAT'S
HEARING IS AT LEAST
FIVE TIMES BETTER THAN
THAT
OF THE ADULT HUMAN.

27. IF YOUR CAT COMES UP TO YOU
WITH ITS TAIL ERECT, ALMOST
VIBRATING, IT MEANS THAT IT IS
VERY HAPPY TO SEE YOU.

28. CATS CAN DRINK SEA WATER! THEIR KIDNEYS ARE ABLE TO FILTER SALT OUT OF THE WATER, WHICH CANNOT BE DONE BY HUMANS.

29. CATS HAVE AN EXTRA ORGAN THAT ALLOWS THEM TO SENSE SMELLS IN THE AIR, SO YOUR CAT WILL OCCASIONALLY STARE AT YOU WITH ITS MOUTH OPEN.

30. CATS SPEND 70% OF THEIR LIVES SLEEPING.

31. CATS CAN JUMP TO A HEIGHT OF SIX TIMES THEIR LENGTH.

32. CATS USE THEIR LONG TAILS TO KEEP THEIR BALANCE WHEN THEY JUMP OR WALK ON NARROW THINGS.

33. ALTHOUGH CATS CAN NOTICE THE RAPID MOVEMENTS OF THEIR PREY, THEY OFTEN FEEL THAT SLOW-MOVING OBJECTS ARE ACTUALLY STATIONARY.

34. WHEN CATS WALK, THEIR HIND LEGS WALK ALMOST EXACTLY WHERE THE FRONT PAWS USED TO BE, KEEPING NOISE TO A MINIMUM AND MINIMIZING VISIBLE MARKS.

Check also:

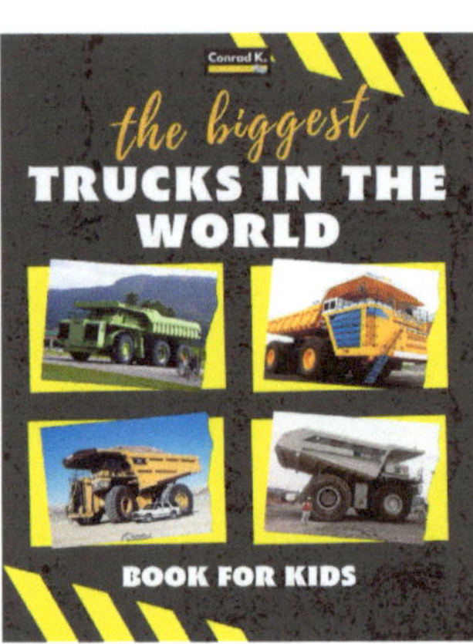

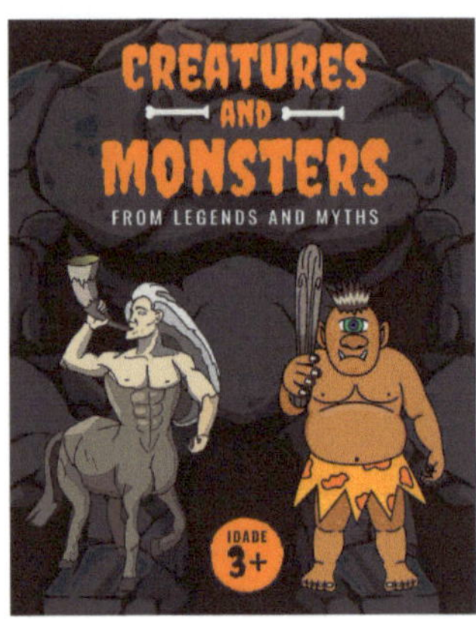

and much more!

www.ingramcontent.com/pod-product-compliance
Lightning Source LLC
LaVergne TN
LVHW071613180726
843512LV00003B/635